AF425608

To Lumi Con Carne & Opo Dopes
-P.O.

To my two daughters, Isabella and Iris
-M.N.B.

Illustrator: Mark Nino Balita

www.loomibooks.com
ISBN: 979-8-9874135-0-0

I'm Loomi
Don't shoo me
I'm not just a fly
I shine really bright
In the day
In the night
I'll help you
I'll guide you
Just follow my light
And never lose sight
Of your strengths that's inside
Your strengths are your powers
These powers are you
I'll teach you
I'll show you
The things you can do
Never forget
To always love you
This firefly will
Forever find you

my character strengths

appreciation of beauty & excellence
bravery
creativity
curiosity

fairness
forgiveness
gratitude
honesty

hope
humility
humor
judgment

kindness
leadership
love
love of learning

perseverance
perspective
prudence
self-regulation

social intelligence
spirituality
teamwork
zest

24 super powers that make me the best me!

Loomi likes to hide. Keep an eye out for Loomi throughout the book!

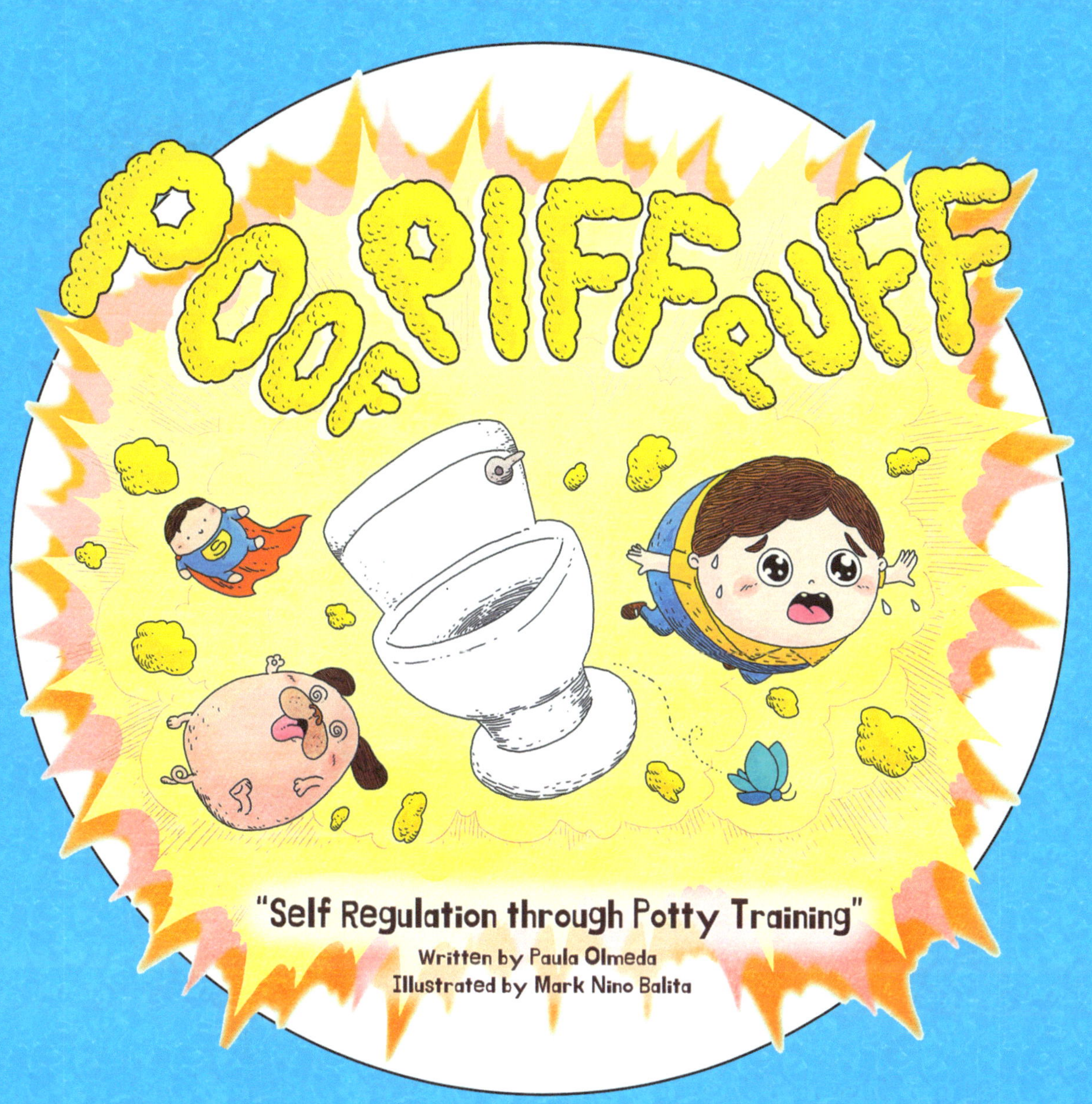

POOP IFF PUFF
"Self Regulation through Potty Training"
Written by Paula Olmeda
Illustrated by Mark Nino Balita

SELF-REGULATION

"I control my BIG feelings & actions all by myself"

What to do when I have BIG feelings

ZZZ...
Opo has to potty.
Opo doesn't like to go potty.
I will help my friend.

You try!
Take a breath
Oh no, oh no!

zzz...
L
I
M
O
O
S
hello down low

You stay inside
or else they'll know
You try!
Find a Solution

Now now lil' guy, you listen to me!
I'm not ready to go, I don't want to potty!

POOF
PIFF
PUFF
M
L
I
O

You try!
Count to TEN
Did that come from me?

I'm not ready to go, I don't want to potty.

POOF
PIFF
POOF

That did come from me!

Now I have to go, I have to potty

Oh no, oh no, my favorite pair,
my favorite pair of underwear.
Do I dare go poop in there?
my coolest big kid underwear?
You try!
Shout
I CAN DO HARD THINGS!

Tip toe, tip toe,
poof piff, poof puff
Poof... piff... puff...

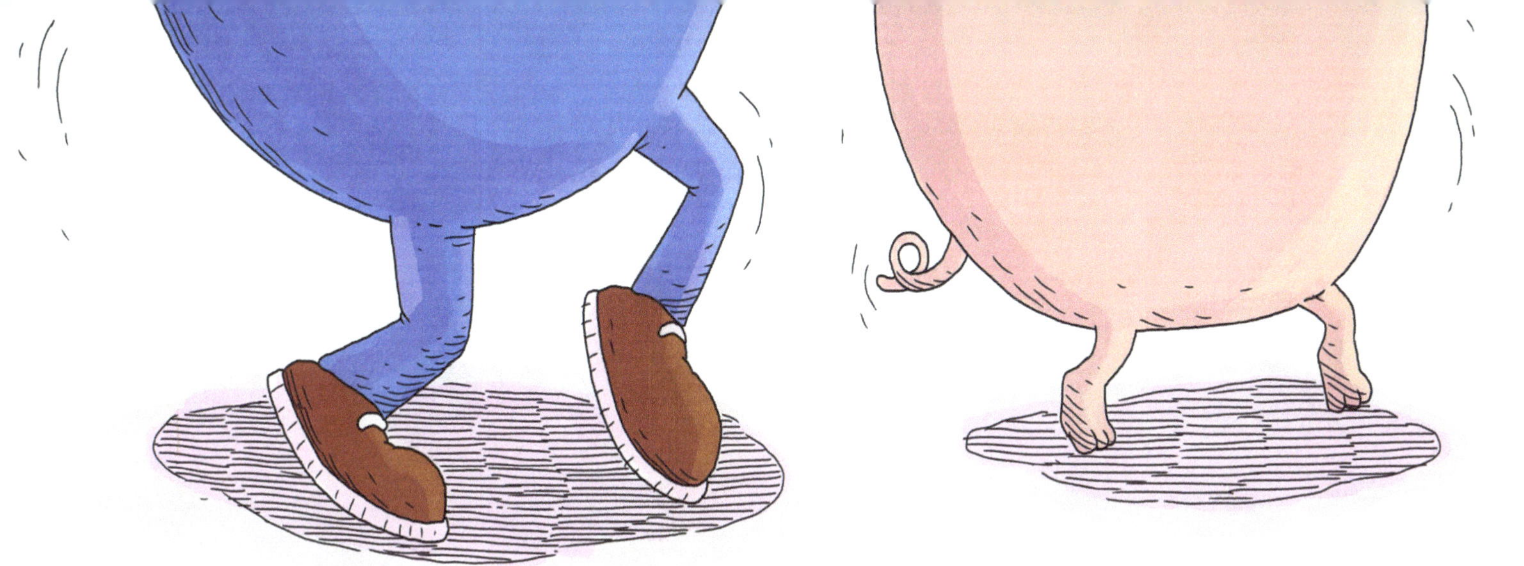

Tip toe, tip toe,

run, run, run, run

hold it, hold it

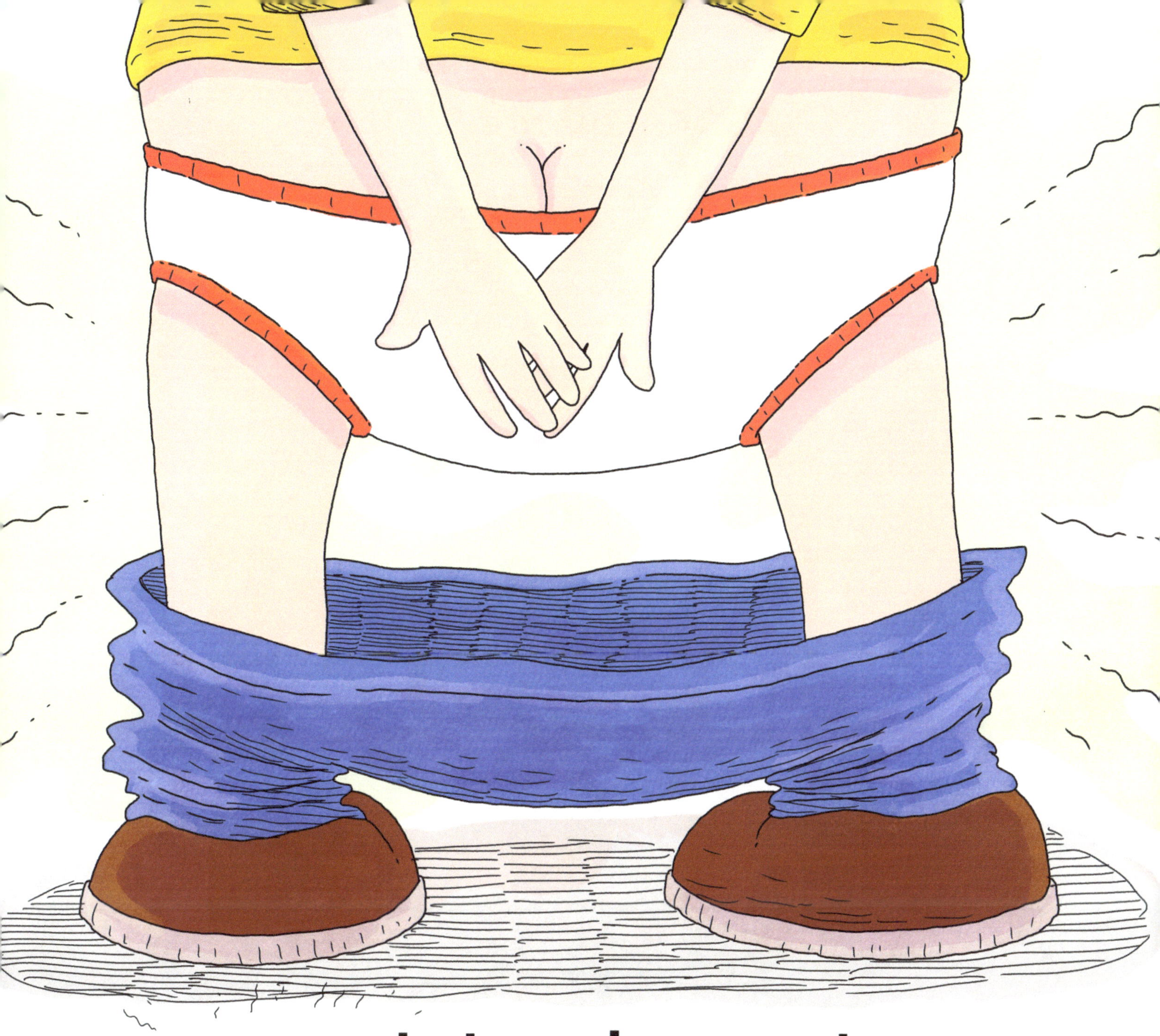

squeeze the bum, almost ready...

yay... all done!
You try!
Shout
I CAN DO HARD THINGS!